LET'S CALL IT HOME

The Poiema Poetry Series

Poems are windows into worlds; windows into beauty, goodness, and truth; windows into understandings that won't twist themselves into tidy dogmatic statements; windows into experiences. We can do more than merely peer into such windows; with a little effort we can fling open the casements, and leap over the sills into the heart of these worlds. We are also led into familiar places of hurt, confusion, and disappointment, but we arrive in the poet's company. Poetry is a partnership between poet and reader, seeking together to gain something of value—to get at something important.

Ephesians 2:10 says, "We are God's workmanship . . ." *poiema* in Greek— the thing that has been made, the masterpiece, the poem. The Poiema Poetry Series presents the work of gifted poets who take Christian faith seriously, and demonstrate in whose image we have been made through their creativity and craftsmanship.

These poets are recent participants in the ancient tradition of David, Asaph, Isaiah, and John the Revelator. The thread can be followed through the centuries—through the diverse poetic visions of Dante, Bernard of Clairvaux, Donne, Herbert, Milton, Hopkins, Eliot, R. S. Thomas, and Denise Levertov— down to the poet whose work is in your hand. With the selection of this volume you are entering this enduring tradition, and as a reader contributing to it.

—D.S. Martin
Series Editor

LET'S CALL IT HOME

Poems

LUKE HARVEY

CASCADE *Books* • Eugene, Oregon

LET'S CALL IT HOME
Poems

Poiema Poetry Series

Copyright © 2024 Luke Harvey. All rights reserved. Except for brief quotations in critical publications or reviews, no part of this book may be reproduced in any manner without prior written permission from the publisher. Write: Permissions, Wipf and Stock Publishers, 199 W. 8th Ave., Suite 3, Eugene, OR 97401.

Cascade Books
An Imprint of Wipf and Stock Publishers
199 W. 8th Ave., Suite 3
Eugene, OR 97401

www.wipfandstock.com

PAPERBACK ISBN: 979-8-3852-1070-1
HARDCOVER ISBN: 979-8-3852-1071-8
EBOOK ISBN: 979-8-3852-1072-5

Cataloguing-in-Publication data:

Names: Harvey, Luke, author.

Title: Let's call it home : poems / by Luke Harvey.

Description: Eugene, OR: Cascade Books, 2024 | Poiema Poetry Series | Includes bibliographical references and index.

Identifiers: ISBN 979-8-3852-1070-1 (paperback) | ISBN 979-8-3852-1071-8 (hardcover) | ISBN 979-8-3852-1072-5 (ebook)

Subjects: LCSH: subject | subject | subject | subject

Classification: CALL NUMBER 2024 (paperback) | CALL NUMBER (ebook)

VERSION NUMBER 08/22/24

For Gracie, Emerson, and Eden, who are as close to home as I'll come in this in-between.

Contents

I. LULLABIES OF ASCENT

Come | 2
Learning to Crawl | 3
Provisional | 4
Tuesday Morning, Thirtieth Week of Ordinary Time | 5
Extra Terrestrial | 7
Stepping Stones | 8
Beneath the Mountain | 9
Holy Mountain Trail Head | 10
Hill Country | 11
Somewhere | 13
Rabbit Trails | 15
Another Week, Another Meal | 16
Not Flat Yet | 18
Pater Noster | 19
One More Day | 20
Catching Up | 21
Ithaka | 23
The Road Back | 24
Driveway Prayer | 25
Know What I'm Sayin'? | 27

II. SPIRITUS VERTIGINIS

The Kingdom: Brief Notes | 30
Blind, Kind of | 31
Revealing, Re-veiling | 32
Word-Hollows | 33
Compost Bin | 34
First Freeze Pop | 35
Cold Shower | 36
The One We Wake At Night For | 37
Becoming Wholly Fool | 38
Over the Know-Ledge | 39
After the Murder | 41
Accidental Prayer | 42
Bridge Man | 43
Halfway House on St. Elmo Ave | 44
Beneath the Landlord | 45
Back and Forth | 46
Higher Elevations | 47
Grounding | 48
Sunrise this Morning | 49
Before the Bell | 50
7th Period | 51
How to Return from the Knowing Place | 52
Further Fields | 54
Practically Speaking | 55
Intimacy | 56

III. RETURNING (LET'S CALL IT) HOME

Sheds, Chicken Coops, Greenhouses | 58
Some Assembly Required | 59
Surfacing | 60
Building the Greenhouse | 61
Weeding | 62

Classification | 63
Common Field | 64
A Handful of Takeaways from Blackberry Picking | 65
Depositing Worms in the Compost Bin | 66
Drafting a Will at 29, Just in Case | 67
Redefinition | 69
Pureed Peas and Other Sacraments | 70
Till it Shines | 71
In Whom We Live and Move | 72
Holly | 73
Increasingly Cranky | 75
Before the Symphony | 76
Sermon, Back Down the Mount | 77
Creek-Walk Epistle | 79
Self-Talk | 81
Waiting in Line | 82
Missing Piece | 84
Coming, Coming | 86
The Angel of Death Veers Right | 88
Encouragement for the Living Dead | 89
Kinda Dead, Kinda Eternal | 91
Discovering What's at Stake | 92
Let's Call it Home | 94
One-Sided Conversation with a 16-month old | 95

Acknowledgments | 97
Other Books in the Poiema Poetry Series | 99

I. LULLABIES OF ASCENT

"Uphill? Or up into the heavens? Let's go, let's stumble and stagger."—Aleksandr Solzhentizyn

Come

Here is a torrential invitation
soaking everything down to the earth-

worms, whose emergence from the dirt
remains an enigma even to the experts

at the Earthworm Society
of Britain, who admit in the fine print

that "though there are a few
theories, it is not fully under-

stood why earthworms come
up to the surface during rain."

Theirs is a sullen acceptance
of what remains both beyond us

and deep in our roots, given
that theories of all sorts have proven

to consistently come up
short of adequate explanation for

this odd insistence that—even if
it kills us—we inch our way to light.

Learning to Crawl

The question of her trajectory—
toward? away?—is not the point
today. Movement's the matter,
and the girl's crawling. Slow
and awkward, this slipping

of stasis, but it's a first flicker
from the flint of a father's
prayer that she tender
a blazing conviction
that there is somewhere beyond
the here worth getting to.

Of course, arrival matters too,
as does the course, but not
now. Enough that she believes the light
knifed across the kitchen floor
is tangible, and more,
                    worth reaching for.

Provisional

On Tuesdays we walk together
across the living room, not going
anywhere but still going
in babbled agreement that it's a long
afternoon when Mom works
late, so we might as well make
something of ourselves and walk
somewhere, her arms as trinket-
heavy as my mind, neither made for holding
much with a stability to boast about.

She carries a giraffe, an elephant, a bird,
and I have words and ideas of how the world
works—we laugh at each other
as one slips out and then another.

Like prostrating pilgrims we stoop
to recover each lost provision at the sure
loss of another one, on and on
until suddenly she stops as if realizing
something, twists around and looks
back at me, a step ahead, then drops
her load and spins a series of twirls
like a bubble floating to the surface,

all light now.

Tuesday Morning, Thirtieth Week of Ordinary Time

All Hallows' Eve

Dead deer, already dead,
again smeared a few yards ahead

on the aftermarket grill-guard
of a jacked-up truck in North Georgia

dark. Intermittently visible
in hazard lights, the old man shuffles

to my window, lights, says he's "shook
a bit but other than that ok."

To hear him tell it, "on my way
to the Snak-Shak to get a sausage biscuit

when *smack*," left bumper,
and that was that. A semi punctuates

his words and divides
the deer in half. We turn to look.

At this point I'm late for work
and unclear anymore what

the work is, or if I'm doing it,
but there's a long trail of blood

and a road ahead.

Extra Terrestrial

No band can tune her hair
these days, so we twist it upwards
like antennae. Wound tight and tilted,

they orbit the house like satellites
searching for a signal, strands
fraying out like burnt wires,

and somewhere between her cooking
on the kitchen set and reading
a book upside down you can pick up

a faint transmission. It crackles in
like a wood knife through a velcro pear,
almost clear enough to swear

someone was whispering your name
or a word you've been looking for.
It goes as quickly as it came.

Whatever's out there, it's intelligent
and wants to be heard, tuning
to the frequency of these local channels.

Stepping Stones

> *"in the house of my pilgrimage."—Psalm 119:54*

The floor—as I trust we're all
aware—is lava. I needn't tell you,

then, that getting from here
to there will require unheard of

feats of creativity from
those of us yet exiled in the living

room, will necessitate we make
daring combinations of the stuff

available. Ours is a bric-a-brac
path we craft one tip-toe at a time,

balancing on what we have
while reaching for what we don't,

imagining our careful way across
the wide floor-plan of our sojourn.

Beneath the Mountain

In the shallow hollow
where Old Highway 2

hits Happy Valley Road,
the radio signal stutters, fritzing

to another frequency until you pass
through, turn, or drop it in reverse.

The reverse may also prove true:
if you find the song that drives you

dropping out, some other melody
pressing to find its way in,

you may be where Old Highway 2
hits Happy Valley Road, or if not

then at some other cross-
roads where you must arrive

at a decision, and based on
how traffic flows, soon.

Holy Mountain Trail Head

Primarily just stay the trail
as blazed. And you'd do well

> (need we say?) to purge yourself
> of surplus weight. Oh, and seeing as

we've got you here, trust us,
don't be over-anxious

> if, on ascending the foothills
> of the Unapproachable

Ascent, you find your
vision start to swirl

> with something like altitude
> sickness, or vertigo. This

is, per nature of the trip,
par the course. Get a grip.

> Don't panic, even when
> your face goes up in flame.

Hill Country

It's a long trek yet
to the town and the hearth-
fire that never burns out,

but "follow me" has a vernal note
to it, singing you along the first mile
like a marching tune,

the woods giving you the green
light and even the crickets cheering you on.
The whole thing rings of recess

and a giggling game of *Follow
the Leader*, when you puddle-stomped
like little rucksack soldiers

and tried to stay in line. But given time
and the steady wear on your soles,
you may begin to wonder

if you're a bit too old
for this duckling endeavor,
and as the weather turns

the lack of visible shelter on the horizon
is—since you're not a duck,
frailer these days and more susceptible

to the elements—troubling. Still,
stay long enough to make it over
the hill and you may experience

what they call a second wind, or
at least a soft breeze at your back
to remind you you're not the one

tasked with picking the path,
though yes, there's still the growing ache
in your chest to reckon with,

that stitch in your side as you
and what's left of our thinning troop
take in the air of higher elevations.

Somewhere

Other than how
                the characteristic
hair-pins and low-
                shoulder switch-
backs serve to
                map something
in you equally
                slow and relentless,
mountain roads
                are also good for
losing things:
                cell service, first,
followed by
                your certainty
that trees are
                just metaphorically
watching, then
                even—stay long enough—
your way, much
                the way this stubborn ache
of ours or a long-
                winded sentence
funnels you
                through its dark arteries
to the heart
                of an overpass
you would never
                have set out

to see, but—
            on looking
back—turns out
            the one place
you needed
            to be.

Rabbit Trails

If I had the pluck, the time,
or rather the pluck to *make*
the time, I'd like to follow

every rabbit trail until I came to know
the many rabbits who believed
it worth their fur to furrow them

through the clover. I'd like this
because I like rabbits
with their diminutive stature,

how even the smallest stalk
is properly appreciated in their little paws,
how at-home they seem on long

winding paths to unseen meadows.
But also because—in my admittedly
limited travels—the paved roads

of the big people advertising
a straight shot to the big answer
have proved something less

than satisfactory sustenance
for this nibbling ache
to slip beneath the fence and feast.

Another Week, Another Meal

The closest I've come to grasping
the meat of this, our one, all-
consuming meal, was at just such
another table, just such

another feast. Sliced heart
of palm, stewed carrots diced
in brown sugar, chicken nuggets
cloaked in ketchup, and she sat

lifted in her high-chair to my right
at the place prepared. At two, the menu
is crowned with a question: *when,*
belovéd, will you accept what's offered you?

There are tears. Morale is low,
so tonight love looks like a slow return
to the table, two more bites
before you're excused, and yes,

we're more than able to sit here till you do.
But even so, were the famine to blow
down the door like a cold wind, not a single
crumb bouncing like a tumbleweed

across the desert of the dining room,
and did the times then demand
such an unhinged spread, love
would lay my forearm across her plate,

or the juicy part of my calf
shaved clean for the sacrifice,
would even stoop to open
my mouth like the gates of hell

and reach into the pit
to extract the still-beating core,
catching the drippings in a cup
while she asked for more.

Not Flat Yet

Nice, every now and then, to see
a fellow acorn-brain making

a good decision. Encouraging
to watch him pause, perk up

and sniff the air, paws tucked
in prayer as he chews over

what the low rumble in his chest
might mean, how best to proceed

with this fresh discovery of a free-
way running perpendicular to his

short line of sight and unfolding forever
beyond it. Good to see him

give these signs their due regard,
and—despite a flinch or three—

forgo his first trajectory,
turning to run *with* the road

wherever it may take him
and up whatever tree.

Pater Noster

Once more she tails him room to room
like the morning tendrils of dream,

blue footie pajamas swishing behind
boot fall. She is all straight lines

and slow pivots, finding at each arrival
the space he just left, faint smell

of coffee breath as he clumps
into the kitchen to pack a lunch,

back to the bathroom to brush, brief touch
as he brushes past to swipe the couch

for keys. Still she follows
like a blind believer, slow

but determined to be picked up,
as if yesterday's *I love you* wasn't enough

to carry her across another long afternoon
of littleness. She totters along,

chasing a father who stays a step ahead,
busy providing for a child

who only wants to be held.

One More Day

Around 7:30 she whimpers
behind the closed door
of the nursery, caged
in her crib. It isn't rage
or fear of abandonment,
because, historically speaking,
someone's always come
to lift her from beneath the arms,
so call it rather a prayer
that this happen sooner
than later, with here and there
perhaps a sprinkle of that fear
of abandonment, because who's to say
today won't be the day
the door knob doesn't spin?

Imagine the excitement,
then, when she hears
the hiss of callused feet, the floor-
board creak. But why imagine,
when you know all too-well
how it feels for something
inside you to be pressed against
the thin bars of your ribs, straining
to hear your name even
whispered, or just one more
glimpse of a shadow beneath the door.

Catching Up

If on a Wednesday, say—call it mid-
afternoon, late September—
you were suddenly to be over-
taken by a vague sense of dis-

jointedness, as if you'd misplaced
something of central importance—
like your car keys, maybe, or a purse—
you'll be glad to find you haven't lost

your mind. This sense is a common
occurrence among those who are—
as *you* are—perpetually a bit scatter-
brained beneath the clock's dizzying hands.

Unfortunately, rifling through your
pockets or retracing your steps
up the slopes of the parking garage
won't recover what you're really looking for.

You left it behind way further back
than you "could have sworn,"
and it's not the kind of thing
that just shows up in a backpack.

In fact, in this scenario, your best bet
might be—the way your parents
drilled you to do if you ever got lost
at the county fair—staying put

until it comes to you. Still, souls
are slow things. As anyone with a significant
other will readily attest, your better half
is nearly never ready, always

lagging significantly behind. So unless
you want to arrive wherever you're rushing
off to, only to pull in with that nagging
suspicion of having forgotten something

important, throw it in park. Idle a bit.
You'll get there quicker if you wait for it.

Ithaka

after Cavafy

Somewhere we got turned
    around enough in making
our thesaurus to render
    'straight' a fitting synonym
for 'true.' No wonder, then,
    that students are confused
as to why Odysseus didn't
    just whip out his handy map
and sail his merry way back
    to Penelope. No wonder, then,
that someone always raises a hand
    on behalf of the class—a sacrifice—
to ask, *wait, is this story true?*,
    thinking to slice like a prow
through the mythical bullshit
    and cut straight to the point.

The Road Back

Even the dog can
               sense the difference,
drops back his ears
               and sniffs the air
as we turn onto
               the street that winds us there.
Asleep in the back seat
               and dozens of turns later,
it's this one that wakes
               a wordless expectation.

Driveway Prayer

Like twin antennae, her pigtails steer
her towards the more elusive things:
bubbles on an April breeze, leaves scraping

down warm cement, the dog bent
low and mischievous, jelly-sandal
in his jaws. She has, in general, little

when she comes to show me
what she's caught, due to slow
pivots when changing direction,

how fast her vision veers for chirping
birds, airplanes, any suggestion
of the word M-A-M-A. Then again,

say she were to find it, whatever it is
she's after—what then? Once
the dog caught a squirrel, lame

in its left leg, and they lay
there looking at each other
in mutual disappointment. If she were

to find you, Lord, as something
other than the faint gleam
of a bubble barely visible over

the tree-line—that is to say, if she were
to grow tired of pursuit and grab
you with her tiny hands—*pop*,

please. Sprinkle her face
with blessing, that she might turn her eyes
upwards, asking—again—for more.

Know What I'm Sayin'?

but she said *what are you getting at,* so I said
it's fresh, you know, like a de-beanie'd forehead
while the ski-lodge croons Lenny Kravitz.
And she said *no I mean like*
what are you after, and I said
it's something sharp, like mint
gum for a mouth-breather, laughter. She went
Luke what are you talking about
and I said *believe me, Baby, I'm trying my best*
to come to terms as our daughter swayed by,
two-year tummy rind-tight
and held out like a melon balanced
on the curved tray of her back,
babbling the thing that's escaped me
since the day I tried to find the words.

II. SPIRITUS VERTIGINIS

"This spirit darkens their senses in such a way that it fills them with numerous scruples and perplexities, so confusing that, as they judge, they can never, by any means, be satisfied concerning them."
—St. John of the Cross

The Kingdom: Brief Notes

Which is more frightening:
the infinite expanse dividing
there from here, or its sheer

proximity, our faces so smeared
with paint we're nearly blinded
to the art? It is, as advertised,

at-hand, *in*-hand, and even—
per St. Symeon—*the very hand*,
if yet concurrently beyond

the grasp of our gouty minds.
With such a far-ranging field
of near-likeness, what might we

then conclude of this kingdom,
this child—prismatic as a poem—
held close and endlessly opening?

Blind, Kind of

Mimi's eyes were fine but she was blind:
a cataract in the part of her mind

responsible for taking what she saw
and knowing it. Genetic, we know

now—traceable up the Coggeshall line,
till leaving South Carolina and crossing

the Red Sea, running through Moses, maybe,
who just once was opened enough to see

a bramble bush and hear what it had
to say. Sometimes I ponder this,

my inheritance. Sometimes I wonder if my daughter,
at two—were I able to remove, like leather

sandals, this skin inhibiting the view—
would now be running around the living room

in a crackling ball of flame. If we're all,
could we take in what we saw, sizzling the same.

Revealing, Re-Veiling

Suppose we surrender the words.
     Suppose, as such, we so obtain
a nearer apprehension of that
     which words eclipse. In such a vein
as this, we might begin to slowly
     ascertain the nearness of the very
pulse we inadvertently estrange
     by means of each and every well-
meaning endeavor to wrangle it
     near, the way inserting a window here
necessitates a wooden frame
     to narrow the view we once
imagined peering unobstructed into.
     Supposing such to be the case,
the chatter stills. We settle here,
     grow acclimated with the presence
which pervades, till breaking under
     the pressure one of us tries to explain,
their breath fluttering the curtain again.

Word-Hollows

> *"the owl and the hedgehog / shall lodge in her capitals."*
> —Zeph. 2:14

Meaning even the ample space
of the upper-case "O" in "Owl"
might harbor one, chin
tucked like an oversized chestnut
or perched in the capital's crook
to leer over the lowers.

This complicates the dialect, you see,
when even the "T" that starts
this sentence might serve as lookout post
for eyes which pry the dark,
some enigma we'll never crack
with our tender hands, our minds.

If true, who else might we find
havening in our word-hollows?

Compost Bin

> *"Take with you words and return to the Lord."*
> —Hosea 14:2

Even if it's across the yard.

Even if they're words as tossed-aside as *earth-
worm, broccoli crown, melon rind,*
and other ends and odd
derivations we find in this pile

of castings we meddle in. Even if,
lifting the heft of such words
on our tongues and the tips
of our pens, we come to the real-
ization that the returning must happen
again tomorrow, and tomorrow.

Even then, when there's no finishing
and nothing to show for our faith-
fullness but a pile of inarticulate
dirt, and maybe, if we're lucky, a few sprouts
we didn't know about, let us return,

opening to the light our few, true leaves
as we dream of a fruit so ripe
it speaks for itself.

First Freeze Pop

On our behalf the high-chair priest
totters into the tabernacle

of the freezer, hands outstretched
for a rolled-up rainbow.

There's a cold flame on the lips,
and suddenly nothing

will ever be sweet enough,
even our tongues stained

when we open our mouths
to tell about it, or ask for more.

Cold Shower

This morning, again,
a micro-rebellion,

a flat stone skipped up-
stream. Again, this morning,

not so much a stick
in the spokes

of the Machine
as a baseball

card, so at least
we hear it coming. Goose-

flesh, brief quickening
of breath—nothing

more than this,
amen,

and once again
tomorrow.

The One We Wake At Night For

The white light scans us
as we scan the shelves ourselves

(4AM: refrigerators around the world.)
And what in the half-awake world

have we stumbled here
in the dark to find, if nothing other

than the flavors we can't combine,
the shadowy craving best called The One

We Wake At Night For?
Rubbing our eyes to pierce

the cloud, we peer to divine
the face of what has called us from beyond

our comforters, the nameless one
that twirls on our tongues

in a place beyond the recipes
and cookbooks intent to seize

and itemize the perfect plate. It is
supremely simple, this elusive taste—

just two ingredients make the dish:
1. Not that. 2. Not this.

Becoming Wholly Fool

> *"So go ahead and holyfool it, dear friend, don't be shy, otherwise they'll all get to you with reverence in the long run."*
> —*from* Laurus *by Eugene Vodolazkin*

When you come to suspect the seriousness
of the sheer absurdity which is
the tremendous tremor of a billion beatific bees
buzzing in the heart-hive, suddenly
you've half a mind to un-mind the other
half, cracking like a hazelnut
the door to the clamped bone cage
of a thousand customs which chains
the starved wildness in you. But halfway through
turning the key you'll remember
your spouse, your children. You did it!
Now you're really split in two!

Over the Know-Ledge

Imagine a shape, a circumscribed space.

Eliminate the edges, then once
again erase those stubborn edges
that your mind—like so much loose
sand—insists on filling in.

Forgive it this bent, this habitual
inclination of fencing in to verify
what's what. It likes to know
what it's dealing with, but for today's
exercise we'll need to exorcize
this hard-wired love of lines
and open the cage if we're to meet the one
we're after, the wildness forever
rattling the brain-box.

Now look at what you're holding. Nothing?
Everything? Are you even sure
you're the one doing the holding
anymore? Hard to see, or say.
On second thought, why
look? If you look it goes away.

Welcome to the turvy-topsy,
your intro course in dyslexic theology
in which you meet the one
in being we whom and move and have.

> *Lord Jesus Christ, Son of God,*
> *have mercy on me, a center.*

The textbook's wild and illegible
as a dog—no wait, a god—unleashed,
so your best bet is to ride it out,
the way you would
when your insides want out
after the roller coaster,
hunched over the toilet
and all of it swirling. (I'm the person
in the next stall over, or I'm the person
rubbing your back. Either
way, you're not alone in this.)

Here's a glass of water, and here are two
consolations to ground you
in this endless opening:

You're over the edge now, meaning
at least what you're careening
towards is a bottomless ground
on which you'll never thud.

Secondly—strange as it is
to use logic here—logically a borderless
shape means infinite centers.

So rejoice: you're yet at the heart
of the matter and always will be.

After the Murder

The crux of the matter is what to do
with the body now crumbled

in your hands. Logic says dismember
it, scrubbing beneath your finger-

nails to rinse away any condemning
evidence of having been at the scene

of the slaughter, then bury the axe.
Or maybe you play it cool, act

like it's nothing new to hold a carcass
in your cupped palms, like really this

is something you do on a weekly basis,
nonchalant as a Sunday stroll. Of course,

you wouldn't be here in the first place
if you were one to listen to logic,

so disregard that. You're holding the flesh
and blood of another. This is no time for logic.

Pray for forgiveness and devour it,
wiping first one cheek, then the other.

Accidental Prayer

> "Come, Victor, with feelings of peace and gentleness that
> will heal, instead of festering, the wounds of our minds."
> —Alphonse Frankenstein to his son, Victor

Yes—Come, Victor, recipient even of petitions
misaddressed to lesser makers, hasten
home to us. Exhume our bloated bodies
from the filth in which we fester. Dust
off our femurs and phalanges, our metatarsals
and our metanarratives of how it all fits
together. Supposedly you've come across
the secret to revive again the lifeless
matter. What's the matter? Our will is fractured
in this laboratory light. Set it right.

Bridge Man

> *"We place ourselves in whichever sphere we wish to be."*
> —St. Gregory of Nyssa

The bridge man looks less like a troll
than I imagined him, though still

plenty haggard, worn thin
as a kite string suspended

between two worlds. His pacing
is not evidence of indecision

but of decision: to make his home here
where the air is thin, where

dizzy, gap-peering pilgrims
could use a steadying hand.

Scott, Robert, Naya, Hunt,
Daniel, Chase, Georgette, Tim.

You, too, can see him. In many faces
he'll be there, here, back and forth

until the bridge collapses,
shores colliding in swift, tectonic shift.

Halfway House on St. Elmo Ave

Observe that the halfway house is—as are
its many inhabitants—in various stages
of disrepair. Impossible to dodge
the smell, the sagging roof. Aloof,

I needn't tell you that
as with any halfway house
its mere existence ought to rouse
(within the neighborhood at least)
a half-hearted effort at amelioration, part
lamentation, part philanthropic endeavor.

Whatever. Look at our bodies, the earth:
when have we ever altered course
on behalf of the passing-places?

Beneath the Landlord

What I'm asking, landlord, is *less*
insulation, actually. Nice as it is

to hear the murmured reminder
of your presence up there,

I wouldn't hate—every now
and then—to actually know

some details of your doings.
Are you rearranging things?

What do you *really* think
of the way we're taking

care of the place? Then again,
maybe it's best we just go on

drifting to sleep to the lullaby
of footfall, pillow-talking our nights

away beneath you, occasionally griping
about what's going on up there

while cutting you a check
for far less than it's worth.

Back and Forth

> *"I'd like to get away from earth awhile / And then come back to it and begin over."* —Robert Frost

From our home in Chickamauga, Georgia,
the city of Chattanooga,

Tennessee is just ten miles away.
This doesn't affect the local day-

to-day. To hear Teri at the Food Lion
tell it, her visit to a cousin

in the land of my commute
all but required a passport.

Still, other than the complications
of tax season and telling someone

not from here where I'm from,
it's best this way. Prone as I am

to drag my feet on the way
out the door, blurry-eyed

and not all that aware, the more
frequent the road-signs

of living in the inter-
state between two worlds the better.

Higher Elevations

Five boys in the house
and a stain-scrubbing saint,
so Dad bought a trampoline
to aid a mutual escape.

He staked one steel pole then placed
another opposite, face to face
like two ancient, immovable anchors
refusing to give an inch, again and again
until he'd raised a modern Stonehenge
behind the backyard fence.

It was only by roots
dug deep in our dirt could we then
stretch the needed tension
tight enough to send us—if briefly—
above our perceived captivity
and weightless in a higher plane.

Then we'd fall back down again.

Grounding

Back then we'd park at the cow pasture, hike
through autumn angst and the thick

excrement of summer, the air
dizzy with fireflies and over there

the State Fair lights. Intent to prove
that I was grown now too—and even *loved*

the upside-down—those nights
I'd run from ride to rumbling ride

inviting vertigo, then sneak off to a bench
when the spin became too much.

Sometimes I still feel the need to ground
myself, the way even the "Hell-Bound"

was riveted to cement. I sneak off these
nights too, slip into the nursery where she

sleeps with bunny draped over one arm,
and touch her hair. How little I am

certain of. How certain the little mystery
curled there, breath steady and circling.

Sunrise this Morning

Every now and then it's good practice
to pause long enough to remind yourself
that you've never really seen the sun

rise over morning coffee. We're the ones
turning here. Stability's a set.
Feel that? You can't, of course,

sustain this perspective for long—
you've a job and family to maintain,
and a spinning brain doesn't lend itself

to a balanced lifestyle. Still,
for a moment consider how effortless
this ability to believe that we're the rooted

factor, this penchant for projecting
all variability outwards, or even—
in this case—*up*. Before you stumble

off to wherever you're going,
turning your face away from the warm stare
which—as it turns out—never

blinks, think about how this changes things
(or doesn't). Among other things,
I guess that's up to you.

Before the Bell

Thud on classroom
glass—a sparrow quivers
beneath the holly bush

while another pecks
his tail feathers
to set him right.

This smudged pane
has us all a bit confused
in late afternoon light.

Legs tick a minute,
like a second hand, then still.
Do we even have time

to find the question?
Still, one perched
on the power-

line decides to sing
a while before following
the rest west.

7th Period

Safe to assume we've got it mostly
wrong, or if not quite wrong
then likely a right that's misinterpreted

the question. That being said, students,
the fact remains that at the construction site
behind the classroom there's a trailer-load

of 2-by-10's used to frame the concrete
foundation that I struggle to believe
they're throwing away. Perhaps

it would be a more advantageous
use of our day were we to spend what's left
of class time shouldering lumber across

campus to the bed of my truck.
I, for one, plan on spending a few afternoons
of my remaining puzzlement puzzling

together a table where my children
can pick up the pondering where I left off,
because I doubt I'll get there by the bell. It's coarse work,

but with every pass of the paper you can't help
but feel that you're getting somewhere,
like maybe, in the proverbial 8th period,

we'll get up from our desks and gather
round just such a table, pot-lucking
a laugh about how splintered it all used to be.

How to Return from the Knowing–Place

circa 3:45pm

Begin by acknowledging the weight
of all this knowing you've been tasked to tote.

Note how taught this tendency
to color-code, file in the proper slot,
how quick you're found to spiral-
bound, staple, three-ring-
bind the unaccounted-for you find
and clamp them in manila cuffs.

Pay attention to the tension
in your spine and other central parts of
you, grown rigid as a hardback.
Now here comes the hard part:

Shrug your shoulders, the way
you once felt safe doing
when you didn't know the answer,
had nothing for the teacher.

Feel the air-conditioning kissing
your damp t-shirt as your backpack slumps
to the floor, more than muscles
loosening as you step inside and drop
it on the mat. You know the rules:

Slip off your shoes. This is what you've been waiting for. All that knowing won't help you here.

Welcome home.

Further Fields

With the scattershot of tractors
left dewing in fields or
on the side of a freeway—

no trailer, median half-mowed—
one has to imagine the farmer
or public works employee simply

puttered out midway through
the back and forth of the work,
clicking the key off to stalk

through the long grass and vanish
to further fields. What's left
are the giant steel husks of all who gave up

the controls with a raspy breath
and took leave of the machine,
their sun-chipped skins reminding us

how tiring our own tilling,
how enchanting the cicada-song
to leave the plow and follow

them wherever they went off to.
We'll do just that, and soon
enough. Today, let's take another turn.

Practically Speaking

Pure and undefiled religion
will run you fifty bones
for a rolltop desk you don't want
but the widow wants gone
because she found him there.

Given that it demands your entire
afternoon, and that it goes so far
as to require you to take the back door
off its hinges, logically
you shouldn't have to pay
the widow to help her lift the weight,
but then the widow isn't
logical right now and neither is
pure and undefiled religion.

What you've acquired
smells like mold and cat piss,
and—wouldn't you know it—
won't fit in the vehicle you
brought to carry it home.

Intimacy

The knee-wall of our prayers
will not contain him in the yard.
Our best translations—

leather-bound—have too been
found incapable of capturing
the nuance of his native tongue

to ears as obtusely tuned
as ours. Unheld, unheard—
how then might we know

this evasive God who is
the right longing we mis-
direct toward getting our hands on

the neighbor's spouse and property?
A pressing question, this,
if one best pondered later, seeing as

the kitchen will not clean itself.
Come: hands deep in dishes,
maybe the answer will find us.

III. RETURNING (LET'S CALL IT) HOME

"And he wondered if being a faithful knight meant that you just went on being faithful without being told things."

—*from* The House at Pooh Corner *by A.A. Milne*

Sheds, Chicken Coops, Greenhouses

Considering that rain, wind, hail,
and various other elements are sure as hell
to warp, and even—at the last—*level*
any feeble structures we erect
to shelter whatever we've managed
to collect, consider these thoughts, too,
provisional. Still, given that
we haven't a choice but raise them
to offer some semblance of order,
and seeing that we might as well
share what's worked for us, if well-
enough, here are a few, small fragments
I've gathered like scrapped
pallets behind Jody's Farm
Supply for the few, small shelters
I've managed—with plenty of shims
and caulk—to raise against the rain.

Some Assembly Required

The hardware provided to hold together
this assembly of ours is small

and hard to hold. We were told,
setting out to build it on our own,

that it would all become clear exactly
what went *where*, but we fumbled

the fasteners with fat fingers
and the thick part of our minds

that can't seem to pinch the connecting
stuff. Screws slip our grip again

and again, in and out, disappearing
in the weave of the carpet, the grass,

beneath a couch, the missing piece
both right in front of our faces

and impossible to find until we climb
down from our ladders and hit our knees,

feeling around like blind beggars
who only discover the point

when it wounds us and spills our blood.

Surfacing

Back in April a flatbed backed in and delivered
a ten-ton hill of gravel that I shoveled,

scoop by scoop, to finish the driveway.
I can still feel the skin thinning

in my spring-soft palms, the reach
for breath as the steel rake screeched and scraped

its teeth on the cold, crushed stone.
It was just about the surface then, and it's done.

This afternoon we sit in the middle of it,
my palms upturned as her little fists

pick up pebbles, scoop by scoop,
to plunk them in my hands, cupped

for the gift. It is her favorite game.
She lifts the stone to place it down again

as something changed, like this is a liturgy
and she's the little priest bestowing me the body.

The weight pulls us down beneath
the surface. We're far from finishing now

and sure to run out of air
long before we touch bottom.

Building the Greenhouse

> *"and then perhaps a deeper memory, a deeper recognition will return."*—Adam Zagajewski

The neighbor swears on the existence
of a foundation, just there,
where the old shed stood.

And believe me, I want to believe
the neighbor and am near-
famished for a place

for something green
to grow in this club-footed,
leap-year February,

but the ground
thaws on its own time,
and the dull flat-head

I'm digging with
brings me down just enough
to scrape against the conclusion

that if a corner block
was once poured it now
abides deep, very deep.

Weeding

She wears my straw hat
and stands at my elbow
like a little mushroom

opening to morning
light. I drop weeds
in her bucket, and she

drops *dirt, bye-bye, flower, house,*
like word-spores on the soft breeze
of her breath. We paint then

with our feet, dark dew-strokes
towards the compost heap,
her hand root-wrapped

around my finger. The hope is
she'll remember this, deep
someplace, grow to love the quiet

unheralded descent, to kneel, to know
the slow work of the daily return
to care for what we've planted.

Classification

Whoever it was, they'd both the gall
and the degree to once and for all

classify dandelion as a weed.
That next summer everyone agreed

their yellow *did* seem a bit invasive,
that come to think of it

it *was* a mite presumptuous to simply
show up uninvited like that, to go

on popping in each spring like everyone
enjoys such calls, like everyone's

just fine with a life they didn't plant
themselves, couldn't buy.

So forgive me my lawn and this lack of fervor
for spray bottles, weed whackers,

and our other illusions
of control. It's not that I question

the existence of flowers, weeds,
everything between—all I'm asking is

that you leave my household out when we begin
nitpicking who gets in the garden.

Common Field

Sure, good fences make good
neighbors, but *no* fences makes good
conversation about who mows what,
because with the easement
where it is it makes more sense
that y'all continue to tend to that strip,
which *we're* okay with as long as *you* are,
and—not that it matters—
y'all know that it belongs
to us, and we *could* plant a garden
there if we wanted to.
No fences compels us to confront
how awkward when our
lives so intimately inter-
sect in this field we share,
how between your family, ours,
and Freddie and Gail on the hill,
we're not as clearly defined
as we'd like to imagine;
how really—mid-gesture down
the blackberry hedge growing
along the property line—
one might come to taste
how silly we sound, claiming to own
even the cluster of words
purpling as the weather warms,
tart and sweet on the tips of our tongues.

A Handful of Takeaways from Blackberry Picking

Yep, the best ones grow
between your property
line and the neighbors'.

They'll shrivel while you worry
about how awkward
it would be if they found
you picking them tomorrow
and asked what you were up to.

Tomorrow will take care
of itself. Love thy neighbor.
Pick them, make jam,
and give them a jar.

Oh, and don't expect to leave
with fruit if you don't give
some skin, a shirtsleeve,
a little blood.

Depositing Worms in the Compost Bin

They might have looked at each other
with watery eyes and whispered

something like "can you believe
our luck?" Egg shell, coffee

grounds, a rotten head of lettuce
steamed in grass clippings, all this

and more before them in a blue
feed barrel, mist slipping through

drain holes with the smell of next year's
vegetables, hot and thick. But more

likely they didn't shed a word
of gratitude or even surprise at their

undeserved fortune. More likely
they wriggled from the palm, falling

to another day of mindless consumption,
shitting on the gift, an act of such callous

defiance that nothing less than long-sitting
love could turn into a garden.

Drafting a Will at 29, Just in Case

To the earth, obviously, my bones.

Preferably in a big wicker basket,
but if someone insists on a box
than a box of untreated wood
so as not to delay the exchange
of goods. Also to the earth
the many poems I pried up
from the ground to call my own.
Just compost them, please,
that they might continue to make
in their breaking till they rise
as sunlight edging the leaves.

To my daughters the chutzpah—
despite lacking the credentials—
to open the hood and see
what's making that clacking beneath,

a love of baseball, the trees
we planted and those we didn't,
neighbors, and everything else
I'm missing which is rooted
and real and too long to list out
or tie down with even the entire
three feet of unfolded cerebellum,
which is another way of saying
the wisdom to shrug their shoulders
daily, staying foolish enough to believe
in lightning bugs and other evening
rumors of light's late-inning comeback.

To the Eternal Exhale I return
mine, and anything good that came
of it. To the Eternal Inhale I go
like the dust to which I've returned.

The rest of you can pick
me clean of whatever's left.
Just close the door quietly when you leave—

the dead, I've heard, are light sleepers.

Redefinition

I wouldn't call myself a prepper,
but I don't laugh anymore
at those who whisper of a dark mass
taking shape, just below
the horizon line.

And have I "drank the Kool-Aid"
if I no longer find
"conspiracy theorist" a fair label
for those who acknowledge
that with so much silt in the water
can we really say with certainty
what big fish is stirring it up?

I don't think "living in fear" is what
I'm doing if I don't teach my children
that we know for sure
what keeps to the shadows in the woods
behind our house, that I wouldn't
advise them to go chanting
beneath a hemlock tree.

And would I be in denial
if sometimes I still go to bed
with a strange lightness,
because by this line of thinking there's
a good chance that it's more
than the carbon dioxide from our
breath that makes the plants
grow when we speak to them?

Puréed Peas and Other Sacraments

Let us not, then, turn
away from even one
of the good things given us
to feast upon, but
actually turn again—
that is to say, *re*-turn—
to receive them much the way
we did when we first began
to eat: without question, so long
as love's hand held the spoon
that in itself held nothing less
than love itself made manifest.

Till it Shines

Unnerving, that day, to discover that Cathy—
my own mother—was the kitchen fairy.

Knowing this didn't make me clean
any more than before, but from then on

there *was*, at least, an aftertaste
I didn't care for when I surveyed my stains.

At the high school it's Rivers, a gap-toothed
granddad immersed in the Good Book

whenever he gets the chance to sit.
Travis and Tina run the night shift.

Come to think of it, I bet the Apostle
pictured us at a cafeteria lunch table

picking at our mush when he asked us
the principle question of whether we had a pass

he didn't know about to go on dirtying the place
(a rhetorical bit he answered on our behalf,

"by no means," probably wanting to add
a few mean words of his own.) Turns out,

it's always taken a real person with a real name
to clean up the mess we've made.

In Whom We Live and Move

We have a large, black dog. This
entails many—if sudden, and brief—

encounters in the dark. This also en-
tails coming to accept that even

most familiar ground—think, the trek
between the pillow and the kitchen sink—

is hounded by a presence. In time,
considering the circumstance, you learn

to tread lightly. Enough collisions
and you also learn to look for him

the way you might a sunspot, a peripheral
form of inspection in which you see

by looking away. All this to say, I've come
to better understand, via the terms

of our black dog, the nature
of another with whom we share

                a space.

Holly

a yellow labrador

One day you'll say your childhood
dog's name and it will sound
a bit odd, *flat*, as if

it were someone else's pet
who wandered like a stray
hair into your mouth.

You haven't thought about her
much in recent years,
but still, you didn't expect

she'd just *disappear* like that,
your mind's silver bowl licked
clean till it shines.

But you can do without her.
What haunts you,
rather, is the crowd of other

constancies milling about your
house, the question of which
will slip out next if you forget

and leave the door open,
even just a crack. The name
of your homeroom teacher?

The drive back, those turns
you know in your bones? And then
what *really* troubles you is how

you'll go on living without them
around anymore. How you
might even do just fine at it.

Increasingly Cranky

Easy enough to wither—
just give it time, and nature.
But to ripen into a fruitful crank
is work: not to chafe against work
or the world, the people who make them
up, but to adore them
more than most and as they ought
to be, so much more so
that when they're anything less you know
the very best that you can do
is make it clear—using words
if necessary–you're not happy about it.

Before the Symphony

As but one amongst the clamorous
cacophony of ding-dongs in this raucous

concert hall, please hear me from
somewhere in the back of the tenor section

when I request—with all due respect
for my fellow brass-blowers and the rest

of you in the thick of it—
could you all just can-it for a bit?

Hard enough to tune oneself
to the quiet note that carries beneath

the discord without all of you
chording in my ear. Are we even sure

what signature we're in? It's times like this
our years of theory stutter, fail us.

Among other things, what we need here
is a little still. Any time now, disheveled

mastermind: Burst through the door, able
to salvage this bombastic babel

into something resembling harmony, and
even—when the curtain crumples—the song

so full we were nearly too afraid
to imagine ourselves a part.

Sermon, Back Down the Mount

"For we are the aroma of Christ."—St. Paul the Apostle

And he said to them—he who knows
the nose's Lazarene ability to rouse the memory,
which is, he thinks, important for his dim
disciples to remember, who have, over time,
accrued on the way a certain stench
to which they are largely ignorant,
their noses perennially stuffed
with the dust they feel inclined to kick up
in every village where they tramp—

anyway, he said to them, "forget the stuff
about the hands and feet a minute.

Be instead the scent of me. Like a high-
school fling's perfume, bring
with you to a room an uninvited
invitation to cast their mind to the other side,
recollect a feeling near-forgotten.

Might they sit up a little, suddenly taken
back to the riverwalk, say, or maybe
the drive in, where they snuck Rosé
in water bottles and love was less abstract, flesh
the evening feature. Might they be unable to wash
it from their mind that night, wake
wondering how to reconnect.

Aroma seems to work the best.

This is my body; take
and reek. Then do a little less
to rinse it off."

Creek-Walk Epistle

To the mosquito-bitten brethren
on this side of things,
pacing as they dubiously eye
the froth and lather of the times,
the scant supply of certainties
protruding from the flux,

Peace. Ten exhortations
of a fellow rock-hopper, slow
seeker of the firm over which
to ford this swollen stream of ours:

    I.
Go, but not alone. The current
isn't safe. We're not
the sure-footed exceptions
we think we are.

    II.
That doesn't mean follow
too closely. It clouds
your vision. Allow a little
space for the silt to settle.

    III.
Our place? Remember it.
Don't crawl or stand over-
straight. Posture is important here.

IV.
Pay homage to the salamander
king whose country we are passing through.
If this feels silly or beneath you,
check that posture again.

V.
Remember that flat stones—
inviting as they tend to look—
are typically slick.

VI.
Get some momentum without knowing
your next foot-fall. At least you're going

VII.
somewhere. So is the water:
somewhere big, and bigger.

VIII.
Maybe it doesn't matter
if we fall in. Maybe we're all carried
there eventually. Then again, maybe not.
Best try your balance on a rock.

IX.
After a near encounter
with a curled-up copper-
head, one mustn't put too much weight
in their right perception of driftwood,
or anything, for that matter.

X.
Still, would that you never
drift in your conviction of a farther
shore, tricky as it is in getting there.

Self-Talk

The words of a well-wisher, stubborn
believer in the efficacy of the Next Thing
to fill the perennial hole,
and this despite returning wholly
hungry from every trite endeavor
to sink my teeth into whatever
hologram fish I managed to haul
with this year's model
hologram reel, eyes forever
on the next hole over
as the place where the real
inhabits the deep, and making a mental
note to venture over there
next week, or maybe even next year,
depending on however soon I can
manage to disentangle this line
which seems to have a knack
for just such tangling. Listen, Jack:

Cut it out. This is
the catch: whatever meat
you stumble upon is a meet-
enough meal, and already wriggling
in your hands. Ever wonder why,
day to day, the horizon shifts its look?
It's a con. Don't take the hook.

Waiting in Line

The line of thinking runs
that given time enough, and the funds,
we might yet get in front of this.

That one day honey *does* the list,
and lo, the fixer-upper's up and fixed,
the lawn at last trimmed low
and all the laundry done, so give
it but a week or so and we'll at last begin to live
the life we always imagined as something more
than a growing list of pending repairs.

Of course, all this can come to pass
only after the ballots are cast,
the offices swept and emptied out
for *our* officials, who will, no doubt,
enact our will and set right the deluded
line of thinking we've too long been governed by.

Then once the baby sleeps through the night—
or say instead the baby graduates
and vacates the house—our ticket
will be stamped to kick up our feet
the way we've always dreamed about
and somewhere along the line
been taught to expect.

So the line of thinking goes,
stringing us along like dominoes
or beads slid down an unbuckled bracelet,
until one morning something shifts
and we wake with a shudder, light
slipping through the shutters to illuminate
the dust in the air as we realize this is it,
that the line of thinking was always bent
until it clicked into a circle,
and—wouldn't you know it—
we're in the middle.

The point is, feel around:
there's no way out of this.
Best start looking up or digging down.

Missing Piece

> *"Let us leave theories there and return to the here's here."*
> —*from* Finnegans Wake *by James Joyce*

You've fallen again for the wiles
of the traveling illusionist
with his winsome "step this way"

bit, that subtle sleight of hand
which leaves you leaning in
to see where the silver coin

of your contentment has vanished
like your spouse in the crowd.
Though you could swear

you kept your vision fixed
on the circling circumstance
of solo-cups, you find

nothing real at each consecutive
reveal but your own perplexity
and a new-found doubt

in your ability to parse out
the hollow from the filled.
Self-assurance sufficiently rattled,

it's then the magician—who,
come to think of it,
looks oddly familiar—smiles,

tilting the cup like a gardener
turning over the turf,
softening the ground enough

that the next part really lands:
a laugh like he knows something,
a petition to take your hand

and reach into your pocket,
showing the gathering crowd
whatever it is you find.

Imagine: the seed of what you're
looking for, right there in your very own
pocket, the entire time!

Coming, Coming

What we're after is just around the corner
of wherever we've arrived. Or,
say instead that what we're hungry for—

the blurry craving in the famished hours
of morning—is not in the refrigerator
or the pantry, unless it's the refrigerator

in the bigger house around the corner.
One might say that what we really desire
is not the flesh of the stranger

on a train, but the tendrils of their odor
as they brush past, smile, then disappear
forever around the bend. We know this, of course,

who have found again and again
the barbecue joint on the other end
of town to be an insufficient antidote

to quell the inner gnawing roused
by the evening smell of wood smoke
as the air crisps and light begins to balk,

who can't understand but can't deny why
something in us wants to take a bite of the baby
in our arms because we just can't hold it close

enough. These metaphors will bring us
close enough, but still, no cigar
will deliver a rolled-tight answer

to the question that such a smell incites
in a cafe, or lingering on a flannel shirt.
So peace to you as we sift through

the pieces for the perfect fit. If you
find me old and still looking for it,
puzzled, please remind me to be patient,

leading me back to bed and telling me
again to sit tight as evening settles in.
The picture will click into place

come morning.

The Angel of Death Veers Right

Getting out, the dog doesn't always kill
the chickens, sometimes settling
to out them from another afternoon

of perpetual pecking
for grubs and other nibbles
veiled within the wood chips.

He's a hound, and plenty quick
for their flightless wings and jurassic
gait—foragers make easy bait.

Instead, he simply buzzes them a bit,
like a robin to an uninvited guest
trimming too close to the nest.

Like church-goers rushing
out the door they flutter in brief distress
before resuming their perennial search

for provisions. He sits to watch—
almost parental—until he's called
to heel inside. He's a simple dog

those days, bent only on ruffling feathers
into relishing this late summer light,
the warmth of his breath

reviving the zest of whatever light
morsels we happen upon,
roused suddenly into tasting them again.

Encouragement for the Living Dead

None of this is going to work
out. The boat will sink,
or the boat will float another

hundred years before
it sinks. The house will uncover
a fix you can't afford,

or maybe you fix the house
and it affords you a dry place
to fall apart, sheltered from the rain.

The garden will gradually be overrun
by rabbits when your fingers
are too arthritic to pull the trigger

of the pellet gun, or maybe
you pull the pellet gun's trigger
and hit a rabbit

who has a thousand rabbit
relatives. The garden will be
overrun. Eventually,

with your consent or without it,
you'll get up one night
or in the morning and wander off

into the woods to see for yourself
where the sound of the waterfall
is coming from. You'll

leave the door open behind
you and the air conditioning
will slip out like a breath

between the ribs. So breathe
easy, friend. You're dead already.
You can never die. Fear not.

Kinda Dead, Kinda Eternal

Try this: when the days attain
the beige hue of nursing-home
couches, flat Tuesday afternoons,

pretend to yourself you're dying
soon. Next year, maybe, or even
next week. You'll know it worked

if the bananas on the butcher block
blast a yellower yellow; finch song
differentiates from warbler;

her passing whiff of perfume proves something
less passing. You know how it is
mornings: in light of the coming alarm

the comforter grows more comforting,
sheets soften as the whole world
fluffs like a flat pillow, flips

like a hot pillow until it becomes again
a place you want to lay your head,
not yet dead. Other times, pretend

you'll live forever. What happens
proves pretty much the same. The beige?
That's something less than both to blame.

Discovering What's at Stake

> *"The psychological trials of dwellers in the last times will equal the physical trials of the martyrs. In order to face these trials, we must be living in a different world."*—Fr. Seraphim Rose

When I hear the hollow thump
of their boots on the front porch,
and that night at last arrives

when they bang on *my* door
with the butt of their torches,
flashing the Empire's insignia

and an eager light in their eyes
as they "regret to inform" me
that it's my turn to be cinched

to the stake, the one that—*yes,
I know*—I picked myself to die upon,
may my children, if still asleep, stir

in their comforters. Let it be a quiet,
cricket-thick walk through the woods
to some thorn-crowned hill

I can all but recognize in the gray
dawn, and when the flames begin
to rise with the sun may my tongue

melt before I can scream out
for mercy. Let it flare up bright
enough that—if for a moment

and from afar—some restless pilgrim
mistakes it for a star
and packs a bag, at last arriving

to the long road home.

Let's Call it Home

It begins by getting up and leaving
the evening's habitual affairs, scraping
back your chair from the kitchen table
and your scraps into the garbage pail,
packing only cupped palms and an empty
Mason jar to chase the lightning
bug that flashed across the field.

What you've begun is at last the beginning,
when looking up you discover yourself
tangled in a thatch of blackberry bushes
enclosing you in a wild, overgrown
embrace, skin traced by thorns.

From this ridge you can see the dim
pin-prick you once called home.

From here you can look back over
the field—still holding the empty jar—
to see how far this faithful,
inconclusive following has led you.

**One-Sided Conversation
with a 16-Month Old**

What you'll come to discover, little
walker, is what we all discover, little
by little. Yes, there's little you can do
to run from the love that wants you. No,
shutting your eyes won't save you
from being seen. It's a slow
trek, this toddling realization
that being caught is the inevitable end,
that like it or not the great *I'm
gonna get you* is the final word.
We're drawing from the boundless here,
way outside the lines—
it leaves us all blabbering a bit,
stuttering for words. Come sit with me
on the bottom step, dangling
your legs like the climb is over.
We're always beginning and already there.

Acknowledgments

To Gracie, for putting down roots with me in the King's soil.

To Emerson, Eden, and any other children we may be blessed with: may these words help guide you home.

To my parents and brothers, whose love is deep in this dirt.

To the men of Muse on Market—Hunt Davidson, Robert Marshall, Daniel Grissom, and Chase Waller—who are the pulse behind these poems.

To Raleigh Gresham, for his relentless encouragement, hours of editing, and consistent reminder that "these poems aren't yours anymore." Here it is, buddy.

To my mentors, professors, and editors—Scott Cairns, Mischa Willett, Jennifer Maier, and D.S. Martin—for their inspiration and their care for both these words and the words of so many others.

Grateful acknowledgement is made to the following journals in which the following poems were first published:

Ekstasis: "Blind, Kind of," "Driveway Prayer"

Delta Poetry Review: "Common Field"

Muse on Market: "Redefinition," "Depositing Worms in the Compost Bin," "Increasingly Cranky," "Back and Forth"

The Poiema Poetry Series

COLLECTIONS IN THIS SERIES INCLUDE:

Six Sundays Toward a Seventh by Sydney Lea
Epitaphs for the Journey by Paul Mariani
Within This Tree of Bones by Robert Siegel
Particular Scandals by Julie L. Moore
Gold by Barbara Crooker
A Word In My Mouth by Robert Cording
Say This Prayer into the Past by Paul Willis
Scape by Luci Shaw
Conspiracy of Light by D.S. Martin
Second Sky by Tania Runyan
Remembering Jesus by John Leax
What Cannot Be Fixed by Jill Pelaez Baumgaertner
Still Working It Out by Brad Davis
The Hatching of the Heart by Margo Swiss
Collage of Seoul by Jae Newman
Twisted Shapes of Light by William Jolliff
These Intricacies by David Harrity
Where the Sky Opens by Laurie Klein
True, False, None of the Above by Marjorie Maddox
The Turning Aside anthology edited by D.S. Martin
Falter by Marjorie Stelmach
Phases by Mischa Willett
Second Bloom by Anya Krugovoy Silver
Adam, Eve, & the Riders of the Apocalypse anthology edited by D.S. Martin
Your Twenty-First Century Prayer Life by Nathaniel Lee Hansen
Habitation of Wonder by Abigail Carroll
Ampersand by D.S. Martin
Full Worm Moon by Julie L. Moore
Ash & Embers by James A. Zoller

The Book of Kells by Barbara Crooker
Reaching Forever by Philip C. Kolin
The Book of Bearings by Diane Glancy
In a Strange Land anthology edited by D.S. Martin
What I Have I Offer With Two Hands by Jacob Stratman
Slender Warble by Susan Cowger
Madonna, Complex by Jen Stewart Fueston
No Reason by Jack Stewart
Abundance by Andrew Lansdown
Angelicus by D.S. Martin
Trespassing on the Mount of Olives by Brad Davis
The Angel of Absolute Zero by Marjorie Stelmach
Duress by Karen An-hwei Lee
Wolf Intervals by Graham Hillard
To Heaven's Rim anthology edited by Burl Horniachek
Cup My Days Like Water by Abigail Carroll
Soon Done with the Crosses by Claude Wilkinson
House of 49 Doors by Laurie Klein
Hawk & Songbird by Susan Cowger
Ponds by J.C. Scharl
The Farewell Suites by Andrew Lansdown

www.ingramcontent.com/pod-product-compliance
Lightning Source LLC
Chambersburg PA
CBHW022121040426
42450CB00006B/788